PREFACE

Design Your Own is a book to encourage children to stretch their imaginations — to design and draw following their own creative impulses. The *Design Your Own* projects are open-ended and there are no right or wrong answers. The purpose of the suggested activities on the back of each page is to encourage and further creative thinking. Many may be done independently, others lend themselves to group research and discussion, and some just present ideas to ponder and think about. Teachers using the activities in a classroom setting may want to write the suggested activities on the chalkboard or on a chart. Students can then be assigned a specific activity from the list as a follow-up to the completion of their own original design. The activities also lend themselves well to homework assignments.

Following the creative process through to its completion is a most influential force in the development of a healthy self-concept. The pleasure and positive reinforcement that a child receives from freely expressing his or her own unique perceptions far outweigh the benefits of a perfectly executed drawing. *Design Your Own* has been created to help a child do just this — to begin with a spontaneous creative impulse and to investigate, invent and present a product representative of his or her own imagination and understanding.

This Book Belongs To

_____

Design your own aquarium.

Design your own aquarium.

- ☐ Look in a pet store or tropical fish book to see all the kinds of fish that are available.
- ☐ Find out how to care for a fish (what it eats, how to change the water).
- ☐ Imagine yourself a fish and tell your classmates or friends what kind of day you would have.
- ☐ Suggest that your class or some friends get a fish and take turns with the various responsibilities.

Design the man-in-the moon.

Design the man-in-the moon.

- ☐ What do you think the moon is really made of?
- ☐ If you were selected to go to the moon and could take only three things with you, what would they be?
- ☐ Watch the moon carefully for a month and record its various stages.
- ☐ Write a short story about a trip to the moon.
- ☐ Find out when the first astronauts landed on the moon. What did they do there?

Design the most beautiful shells in the world.

11

Design the most beautiful shells in the world.

☐ Find out where shells come from and how they are formed.

☐ Make a list of different animals that have shells (oysters, clams, snails).

☐ Start a shell collection of your own.

☐ Draw or paint a picture of some shells.

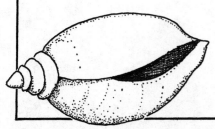

Design a modern nest for town house birds.

Design a modern nest for town house birds.

☐ Draw a picture of the most beautiful bird you can imagine.

☐ What birds haven't you seen that you would like to see?

☐ Make a birdhouse to put in your backyard.

☐ Do you know what birds sleep on one foot? Use a reference book to find out and to learn more about these birds.

Design your own hamburger.

Design your own hamburger.

☐ Write down your favorite recipes made with hamburger meat.

☐ Start your own cookbook with recipes that are your favorites.

☐ Write a story about the world's largest hamburger and what happened to the person who ate it.

Design your own garden.

Design your own garden.

☐ Make a list of all the things you want to grow.

☐ Find a seed catalog and select some unusual plants you would like to grow in your garden.

☐ Draw a picture of the layout of your garden.

☐ Find out how to start a garden — where to buy seeds, tools; what time of year to plant; and how to care for your garden during different seasons.

☐ Start a small garden at school or with friends in your neighborhood.

Design your own graffiti.

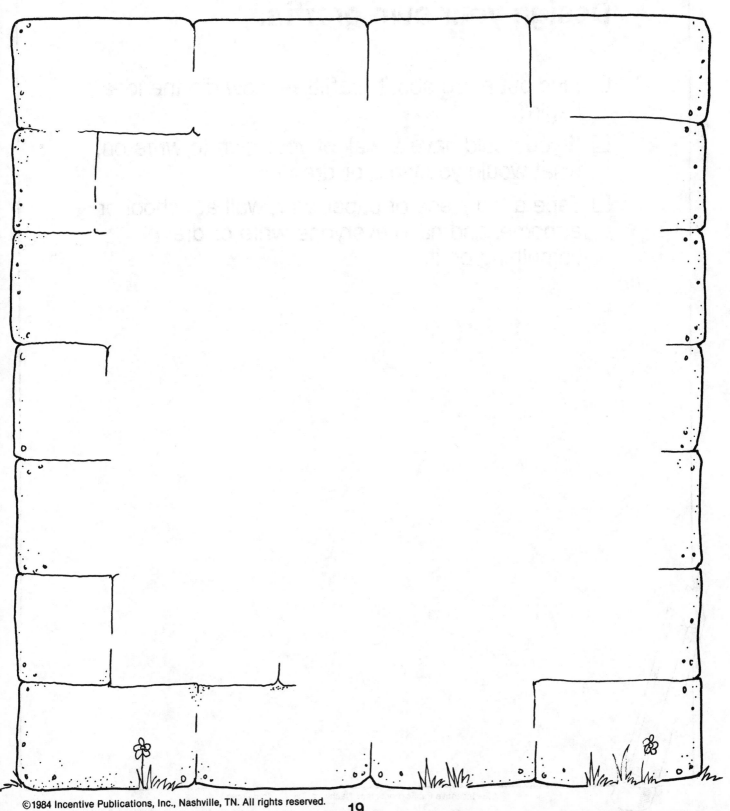

Design your own graffiti.

☐ Find out more about graffiti — how did the idea begin?

☐ If you could have a wall of your own to write on, what would you write or draw?

☐ Tape a big piece of paper on a wall at school or at home, and have everyone write or draw something on it.

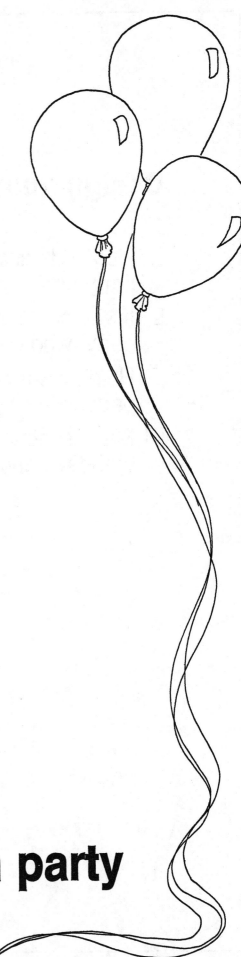

Design your own party hat.

Design your own party hat.

☐ Use odds and ends from home to make your own party hat.

☐ If you could invite anyone you wanted to your party, whom would you invite?

☐ Help plan a neighborhood skating or swimming party.

☐ Make special invitations and favors for your next birthday party.

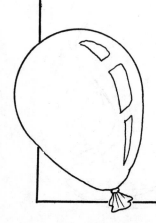

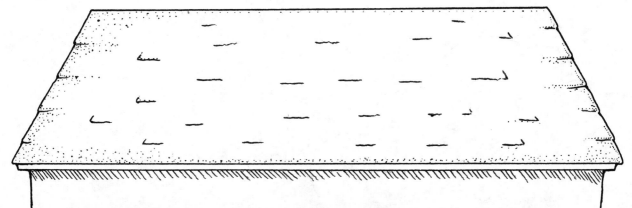

Design a weather vane.

Design a weather vane.

☐ Where would you put your weather vane?

☐ What kind of weather do you like best?

☐ Find out how scientists predict our weather. What kinds of tools do they use?

☐ Put a thermometer outside and keep a chart to record temperatures at the same time each day for a month.

Design your own T-shirt.

Designed by:

Design your own T-shirt.

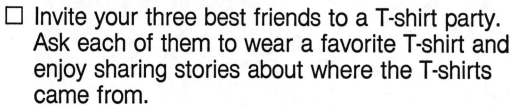

- ☐ Paint a design on a T-shirt for you or a friend.
- ☐ Use embroidery thread and other odds and ends from the family sewing box to decorate a shirt that needs some new life.
- ☐ Invite your three best friends to a T-shirt party. Ask each of them to wear a favorite T-shirt and enjoy sharing stories about where the T-shirts came from.

Design a machine to water all your house plants.

Design a machine to water all your house plants

Design a machine to water all your house plants.

☐ How would the machine work?

☐ Where would the water come from?

☐ Plant some seeds and share watching them grow with your classmates or family.

☐ Plant some bulbs and make caring for them your own special project.

☐ Look in magazines and seed catalogs for pictures and descriptions of house plants you would like to grow.

Design your own forest.

Design your own forest.

☐ Take a walk in a wooded area. Write down some of the sounds you hear and things you feel and see.

☐ Draw or paint a picture of a forest or make a picture from twigs and leaves you find.

☐ Make a maze of a forest and try to find your way through it.

☐ List all the animals you might see in a forest.

Design a nice day at the beach.

Design a nice day at the beach.

- ☐ Make a list of the kinds of plants and animals you would expect to see at the beach.
- ☐ Why do you think the ocean is salty?
- ☐ Look at a map to see all the different places that have beaches.
- ☐ Talk with a friend or classmate about the different kinds of jobs people have on or near a beach.
- ☐ What would you take to the beach if you were going for the whole day?

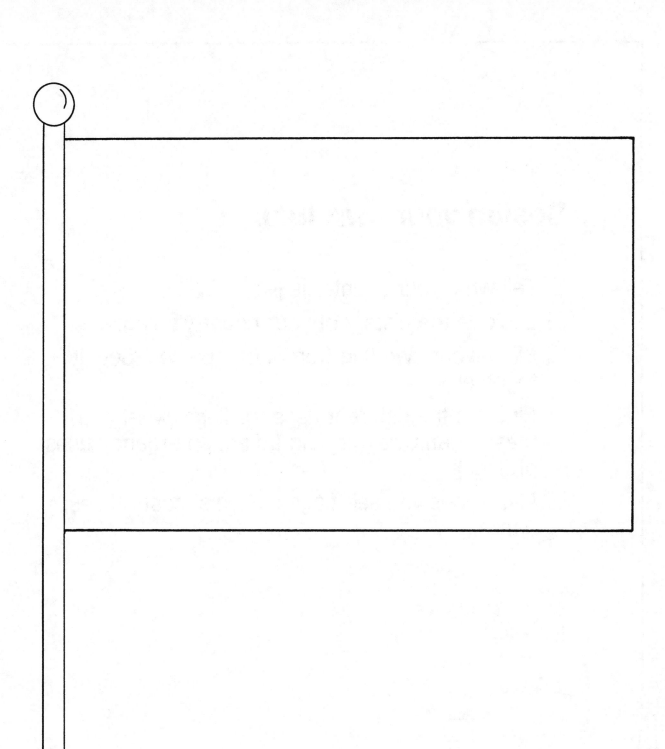

Design your own flag.

Design your own flag.

- ☐ Tell what your country is like.
- ☐ Look up the history of your country's flag.
- ☐ Make your own flag from fabric pieces. Sew it together.
- ☐ Find out the different uses for flags (what half-mast means, how to fold a flag, emergency uses of flags).
- ☐ List places you see flags (schools, post offices, banks).

Design your own castle.

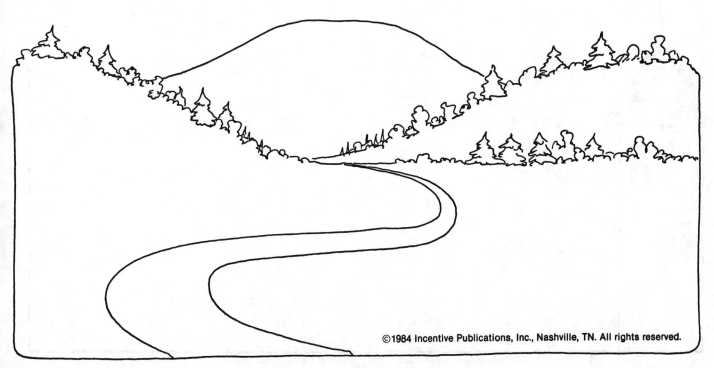

Design your own castle.

- ☐ Pretend you are living in a castle and tell what it would be like.
- ☐ Make a sand castle either at the beach or in a sandbox.
- ☐ At school or with your neighborhood friends, act out a play set in medieval times.
- ☐ How would a castle be different from your house?

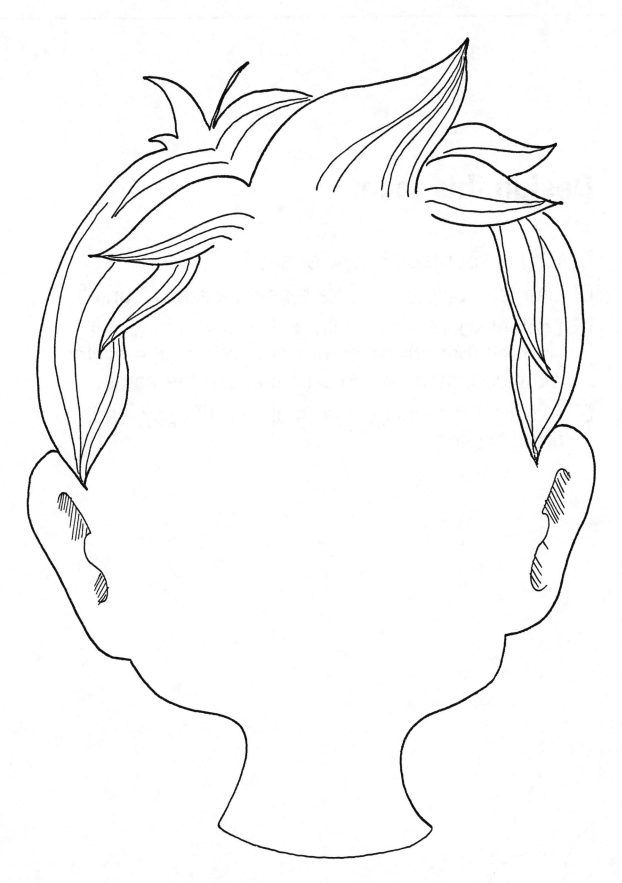

Design this face.

37

Design this face.

☐ Why is your face happy or sad?

☐ Use face paints to make a new face for yourself.

☐ Look at yourself in a mirror. List features about yourself that are different from your brother/sister/mom/dad, then list features that are the same.

☐ Make a list of things that make you happy, sad, tired, excited.

Design your own house.

Design your own house.

- ☐ Cut out pictures from magazines of houses you like and make a collage or a book of houses.
- ☐ Write down the things you like best about your own house and room.
- ☐ What steps are taken in building a house?
- ☐ Make a list to compare different types of houses (igloos, tepees, barns).

Design your own record album cover.

Design your own record album cover.

☐ Pick out some of your favorite records and share them with your class or friends.

☐ Look in an encyclopedia to see how records are made.

☐ Listen to music with your eyes closed and write down some of the instruments you hear.

☐ Make your own instruments from things at home (spoons, boxes, combs) and have some friends get together for a jam session.

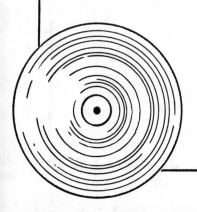

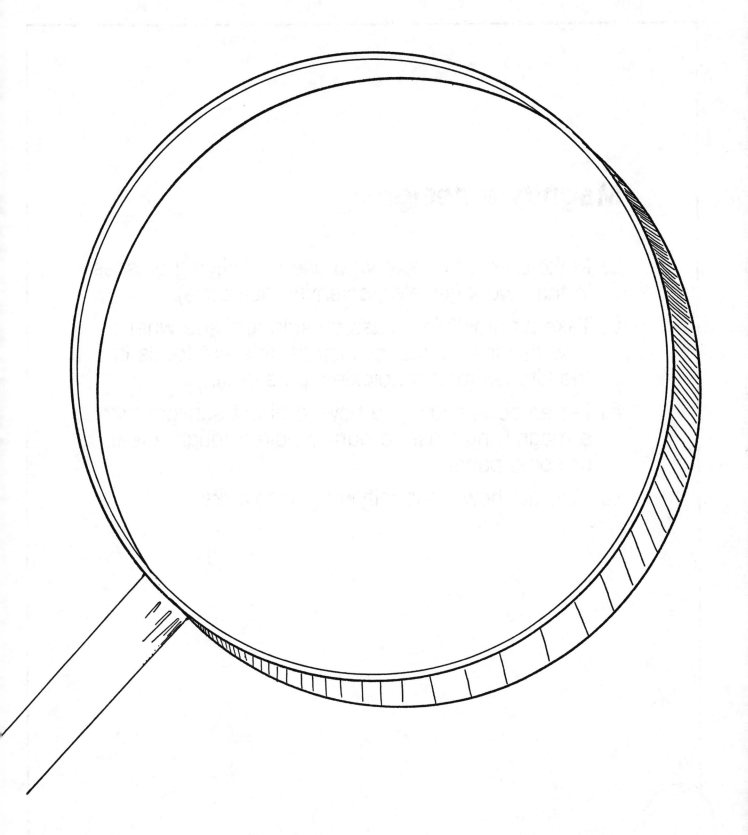

Magnify a design.

Magnify a design.

☐ Make a list of people who use magnifying glasses in their work (jeweler, scientist, detective).

☐ Take a magnifying glass outside and see what new things you see, or look at different foods in the kitchen (onions, pickles, potatoes).

☐ Let an adult show you how to direct sunlight with a magnifying glass to burn a hole through a leaf or some paper.

☐ Find out how a magnifying glass works.

Design your own school bag.

Design your own school bag.

☐ Find a paper bag and color a design on it.

☐ Make a list of other types of school bags (baskets, satchels, backpacks).

☐ What would you put in your bag?

☐ Where would you keep it?

☐ Sew your own bag at home for the school year.

Design your own sunglasses.

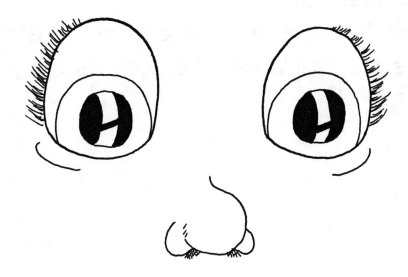

Design your own sunglasses.

☐ Where would you wear them?

☐ Make a pair of sunglasses from heavy paper and decorate them.

☐ What is your favorite shape for sunglasses?

☐ Design a special pair of sunglasses and give them to a friend.

Design a machine to help a bee make honey.

Design a machine to help a bee make honey.

☐ Look up bees in an encyclopedia to see how they *do* make honey.

☐ Write down five good ways to use honey.

☐ Trade recipes containing honey with a friend.

☐ If you were a bee, where would you go to make your honey?

What's on the branch?

What's on the branch?

☐ Investigate a branch from a tree — cut it in half, notice the bark and the leaves.

☐ Draw the branch you sit on in your favorite tree.

☐ Find out how certain insects camouflage themselves to look like branches.

☐ Look up different ways trees are used (wood to burn, paper, construction).

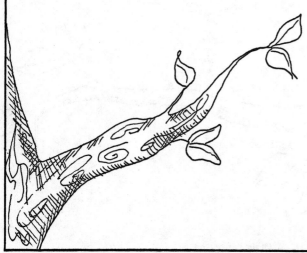

Design a computer to do your homework.

Design a computer to do your homework.

☐ What subject would you have the computer do for you?

☐ List the kinds of things your computer can do (add, subtract, spell).

☐ Find out how computers are changing the way we live.

☐ Make a list of ways you think a computer could help your family.

Design a one-person band.

Design a one-person band.

☐ Get together with friends at school or in your neighborhood and play different instruments.

☐ Draw a picture of someone who is a one-person band, and tell what instruments he or she plays.

☐ Make up a story about a group of animals that form a band.

☐ Ask your friends at home or at school what instruments they play.

Design some companions for this whale.

Design some companions for this whale.

☐ Look up whales in the encyclopedia to find out where they live and what they eat.

☐ Make a whale from two pieces of felt. Stuff it with cotton, beans or rice.

☐ Write a story about a whale.

☐ Find out what other fish live in the same waters with whales.

☐ Find out whom you can write to help protect whales.

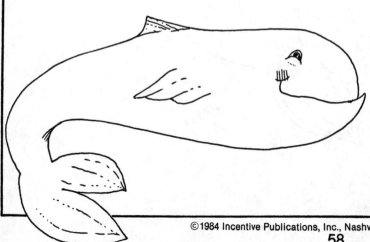

Design the habitat.

Design the habitat.

- ☐ Discuss your own habitat with your family.
- ☐ Find out how penguins are adapted for cold climates.
- ☐ Write a short story about a penguin named Patrick.
- ☐ Make a penguin puppet.
- ☐ Draw a picture of a new habitat for yourself.

Design your own sailboat.

Design your own sailboat.

☐ If you could sail away, where would you go?

☐ Write a story about a real or make-believe adventure on a sailboat.

☐ Use popsicle sticks or toothpicks and some glue to make a boat.

☐ Find out some differences between sailing and motorboating.

Design your own lettering.

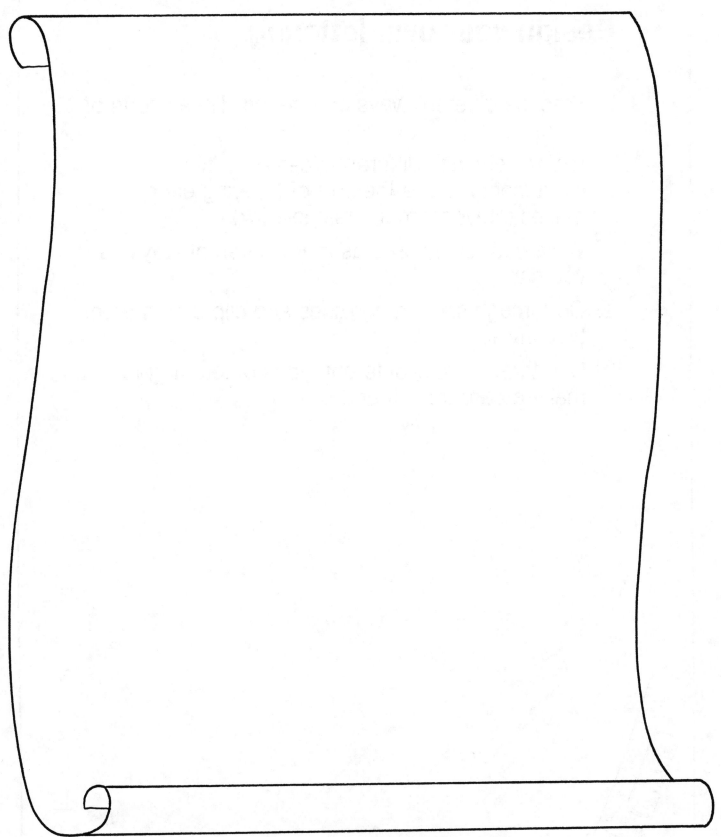

Design your own lettering.

☐ Practice different ways of lettering. Try all sorts of styles.

☐ Experiment with different types of writing instruments to see the sort of lettering each makes (crayons, markers, India ink).

☐ Write your own name as many different ways as you can.

☐ Go through some magazines and clip out different type styles.

☐ Use three or four different types of lettering to make a card for a friend.

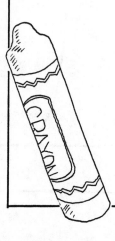

Design your own cowboy boot.

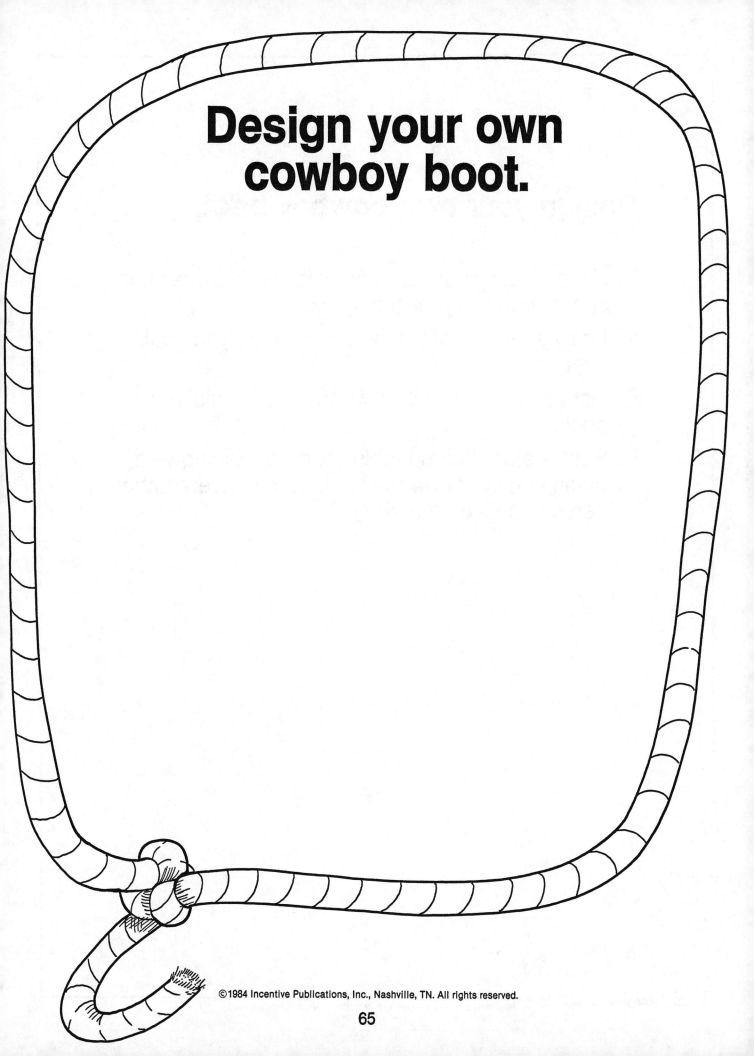

Design your own cowboy boot.

☐ Keep a record of your shoe size over a year and see how much your feet grow.

☐ Draw a picture of the greatest shoes you could ever own.

☐ List places or activities where you should wear boots.

☐ Start a story "round-robin style" beginning with putting on your cowboy boots, then have another person continue the story.

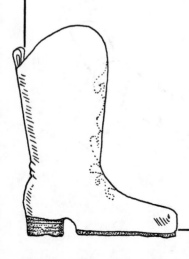

Design your own notepaper.

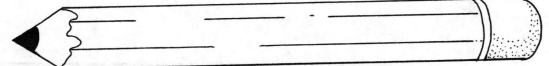

Design your own notepaper.

☐ Pick out some plain stationery. Paint or draw a design on a few pages and write letters to friends or relatives.

☐ If you could receive a letter from anyone in the world, who would that person be?

☐ Investigate a pen-pal friendship with someone in another state or country, and start your correspondence.

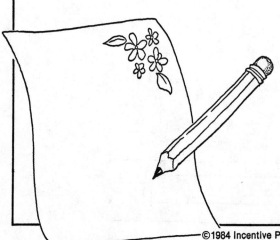

Design a quilt showing some of your favorite things.

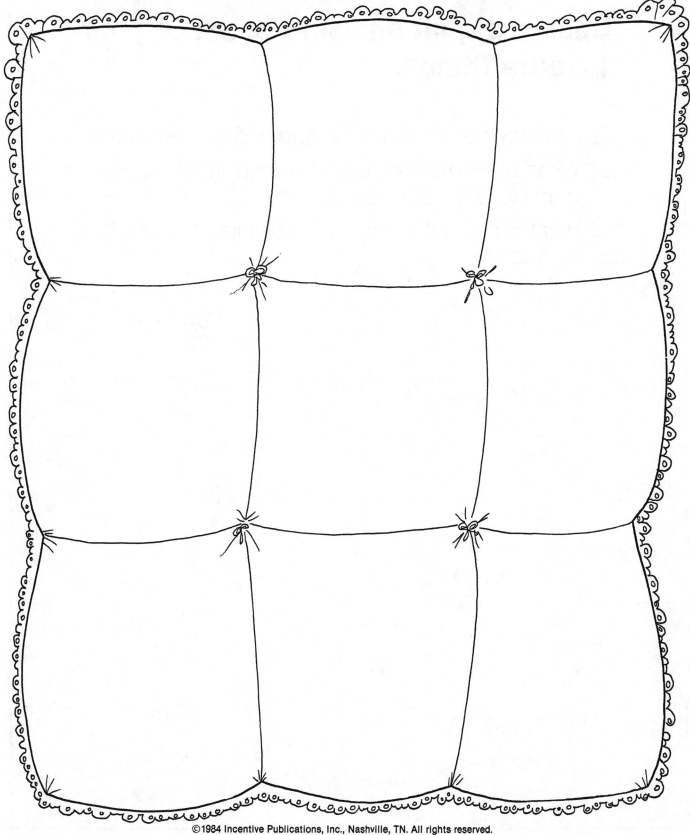

Design a quilt showing some of your favorite things.

☐ Look up the art of quilting and find out its history.

☐ What is the most important or exciting thing that is included in your quilt design?

☐ What is it about your favorite blanket that you like so much?

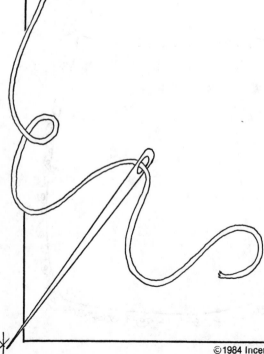

Design an envelope seal.

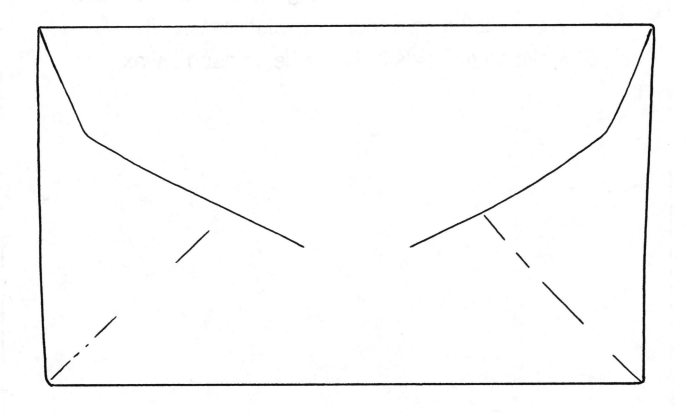

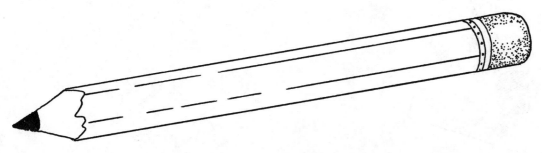

Design an envelope seal.

☐ Make up other designs for your family and friends — they make great gifts.

☐ Try different seals using your name, initials or favorite things — something that represents you.

☐ Write a letter to a friend or relative. Seal it.

☐ Make some seals at home using candle wax.

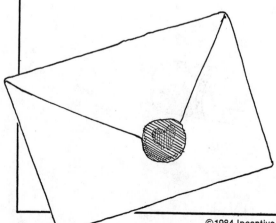

Design your own treasure box.

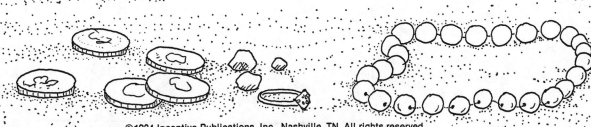

Design your own treasure box.

☐ Write a story about your treasure box. What's inside it?

☐ Find a box at home, paint it or draw on it, and fill it with your favorite things.

☐ Find out what kinds of real treasure chests have been found.

☐ Make a list of all kinds of uses for boxes.

☐ Make a treasure box for a friend for a birthday present.

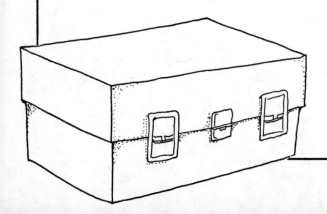

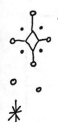

Design a snowstorm.

Design a snowstorm.

☐ Draw a picture of the snowman you would build if there were fifteen inches of snow.

☐ Find out how animals stay warm in the winter.

☐ What is your favorite activity to do in the snow?

☐ Use a reference book to find out what weather conditions cause snow to fall.

Design a label for your favorite food.

Design a label for your favorite food.

☐ What is it about your favorite food that you like so much?

☐ What important items are listed on cans you have at home (weight, ingredients, price)?

☐ Have a family discussion about food shopping, and see if you can help with a grocery list.

☐ Make up a recipe with your favorite food in it.

Design yourselfe in days of olde.

Design yourselfe in days of olde.

☐ What kinds of chores would you have had to do fifty years ago?

☐ If you could be a famous person who lived a long time ago, whom would you like to be?

☐ What do you think is the best thing about living in the time period we live in now?

☐ Draw a picture of what you think you'll look like in twenty-five years.